Tickles the Bear

By Marcel Pighin

Illustrated by Irma Daggett and Marcel Pighin

All Rights Reserved. Copyright © 2000 Marcel G. Pighin

No part of this book may be reproduced or transmitted in any form or by any means, graphic, electronic, or mechanical, including photocopying, recording, taping or by any information storage or retrieval system, without the permission in writing from the publisher.

Published by MP2ME Enterprise
For information, please contact:

MP2ME Enterprise
16754 SE 45th Street
Issaquah, WA 98027
http://www.mp2me.com

ISBN: 0-9717947-5-8

Printed in the United States of America

To my inspirations,
My daughters.

Table of Contents

Table of Contents	4
Introduction	5
How Tickles Came To Be	7
Snowball Is My Friend	11
Alone At Home	17
Tickles Goes To The Circus	21
Tissue Paper	27
Tickles Is Lost!	31
Pizza Contest	39
Snow!	51
Toby	59
Sing A Song!	64
Feet!	72
Friends From Far Away	78

Introduction

Tickles was a bear.
He lived each day without a care.
His motto, so they say,
Was play, play, play all day, day, day!

How Tickles Came To Be

How did Tickles become a bear
That lived each day without a care?
A small, little bear with so much zeal,
Wendy's parents said, "Thank goodness he isn't
real!"
As Wendy imagined, it happened this way,
Up north, before Christmas, in Santa's Workshop,
one day.
A mischievous elf that was working aplenty.
The elf had made one small, white bear too many!
"All the same,
All so white and plain."

"To this cute little guy I must add a spark!"
The elf sewed a bright, blue spark within a bright
red heart!
We all know sparks are hot and bright—
Full of life.
That is how the bear became Wendy's Tickles on
that night.

<u>Snowball Is My Friend</u>

After being created by a mischievous elf,
Before Santa delivered Tickles to Wendy's house—
himself,
Tickles ran off.
Out the door he did go—
Out the door and into the snow!
With a shriek of delight
At the beautiful sight,
Tickles walked up a hill— not very fast.
He followed a path.
At the top of a hill, he could see all around.
Tickles shrieked, once again, at a friend he had
found.

A little round penguin about the same size as
himself,
Tickles decided to go down the hill to find out the
penguin's name.
"Could it be Samantha, Srini, or Ralph?"
"Hello!" he said, "Tickles is my name."
"Hello!" the penguin said, "My name is Snowball,
Do you want to play a game?"
Tickles said, "I have never played a game before."
Snowball said, "Playing no games would be an
awful bore."
"I will teach you to play!
What do you say?"

So, up the hill in the snow,

The small penguin and bear did go.

Snowball had borrowed a small, gift box from

Santa's shop.

Tickles pulled and Snowball pushed the box up the

hill— to the top.

"Hop in the box— now!" Snowball said.

Snowball pulled down the wool stocking cap, tight,

upon his head,

"We are ready to slide!"

Tickles jumped in, ready to ride!

With a push and a shove by the penguin above,

Snowball jumped in too!

The game was to ride down the hill and yell

"Yahoo!"

Tickles said, "Yahoo! Yippee! This is fun!"
All too soon they were done.
They went up the hill, once again.
Up the hill and down the hill until their rides
counted ten.
Tickles said, "I could play, play, play,
All day, day, day!"
But in the end,
With his friend,
Back to Santa's workshop they did go.
Out of the cold and out of the snow.

An elf saw them come in.
The elf carried them to a toy bin.
This is where they waited for the day
When Santa would come to take them away,
To Wendy's house, to play, play, play!

Alone At Home

The Feldoon family was away,
Tickles was left at home to play—
As he did on every other day.
He went upstairs, to Wendy's room.
Tickles wanted to see if he could play a tune.
Doll clothes were everywhere.
Tickles put them on without a care—
Dressing in things I would not dare.
He said to himself, "A tune to dance,
In the finest clothes this side of France!"

He put on a tune and jumped on the bed.
Tickles danced and jumped, and stood on his head.
He frolicked around for an hour or so.
Tickles thought to himself, "No one else will know!"
All of a sudden he heard a noise.
Maybe it was just one of Wendy's toys.
"Oh No! The family is home! I cannot dance.
They are going to see me in these fancy pants!
What to do, I do not know.
Lie on the bed— lie low, lie low!"

Wendy came into her room singing a song.
The song had been stuck in her head all day long.
She saw Tickles lying on the bed in clothes, by chance.
The finest she had seen this side of France!
She picked up Tickles and jumped on the bed.
She danced, with Tickles, to the tune that had been stuck in her head.
Somehow,
The tune was playing, right now,
On her music player— near the foot of her bed.

Tickles Goes To The Circus

Tickles said, "Today will be special!
Today will be great!"
Wendy's parents said Tickles could come to the
circus with Wendy—
They were running a little late.
Wendy picked up Tickles and they went.
They arrived at the circus and sat down inside a
great striped tent.
There were lions and trapeze artists too!
Tickles wondered if they had borrowed the animals
from the zoo.

The trapeze artists were swinging so high—
Almost touching the sky.
At that moment, just then,
Wendy imagined her little friend, Tickles, sneaking
off around the back of the tent.
This was where the clowns were getting ready for
the big event!
The clowns saw Tickles and laughed full of glee.
We will have a bear clown! Let us hurry and get
him ready!

The clowns painted Tickles face yellow—
A strange color for a white, furry fellow.
"Do not worry," said the clowns, "the paint will come off in a jiff."
Upon Tickles' nose they placed a bright red gift.
It was a red clown nose. Tickles was ready to go!
"Let's get on with the show!"

Tickles was a hit! He jumped and he flipped.
The clowns were all silly. They danced and they tripped.
All great events must come to a close.
Tickles bowed to the crowd.
A clown bopped Tickles on the nose—
Just once, as he rose.
The crowd laughed and they giggled.
For now Tickles' red nose shone bright and it wiggled!

Those silly clowns had put a light in the nose.
It shone— oh so bright.
Wendy thought Tickles was quite a sight!
At home Wendy washed off the yellow—
Off her small, furry fellow.
The pretend, face paint came off just fine.
Wendy said, "I am so glad you are mine."
She put him to bed and made him all snug.
Then she gave Tickles one last, big hug.

Tissue Paper

Tickles and Wendy played today,
With tissues, on Tickles, in every which way.
Tissue for a hat and tissue for a gown,
Tickles said he looked silly. Wendy gave him a frown.
"You must get ready so we can go out together.
You must wear this fine tissue hat with a fine, fluffy feather! "
"Now Tickles, be still while I dress you!" she said,
"I'm your mommy!
Tickles, be still or I will tickle your tummy!"

Tickles sat still for a second or two.
That was the best he could do.
He squirmed and he wiggled
Of course, Wendy tickled his tummy— they both giggled.
"You are tired and I am tired too.
To bed you must go with a blankey made of tissue."
And to bed Tickles went, at the end of the day.
Tickles was tired. There was nothing more to say.
Tickles needed to rest after dressing up in tissue every which way.

Tickles Is Lost!

One day Wendy brought Tickles into the forest.
Wendy was looking for flowers.
She was pretending to be a florist.
It was getting late but into the forest Wendy went.
The forest was not far from their house. It was a place where time was spent
Quietly looking at the plants and animals that were there.
On this day, Wendy and Tickles even saw a bear!
The bear scared them both and Wendy ran to the house.
She dropped Tickles on the way— Tickles was scared. He lay quiet as a mouse.

Wendy ran like the wind, to the house she did go.
Meanwhile, Tickles was missing and Wendy did not know!
Wendy called for her mom, "A bear is in the forest!" she said.
Horrible thoughts of the bear chasing her were racing through her head.
Wendy's mom came— quite quick.
Meanwhile, Tickles had been forgotten and was starting to feel quite sick.
"Sticky mud, sticky mess—
I must have swallowed some mud, I would guess."

Wendy's mom asked if she was alright.
"The forest is not a place for little girls to go all alone— especially at night!"
Wendy said, as tears swelled in her eyes, "I have lost Tickles! I do not know where!
I dropped Tickles in the forest when I ran from the bear!"
Wendy's dad found Tickles lying quiet as a mouse
Not far in the forest— her dad brought Tickles back to the house.
Tickles was sad. He was a muddy mess.
Tickles was not himself. He was not full of zest.

Tickles felt Wendy did not care
When she dropped Tickles in the forest and ran
from the bear.
"I am a bear, you know," Tickles said with a frown.
Wendy smiled because she was so happy to see her
white bear that was now all brown.
"Oh Tickles," Wendy said, "That bear was not like
you. It was wild and free and kind of scary!"
Wendy's father came into the kitchen, just then, and
said, "I would have to disagree!"
"Oh Dad!" Wendy said "You make me mad!
Can't you see Tickles is sad?"
"I am sorry, Tickles," Her father said. "I take what I
said back.
I was just coming in the kitchen for a snack!"

Wendy said, "Tickles, you are not just a bear to me.

You are part of our family!

I love you, my bear,

And I do really care!"

Tickles heart was filled with glee—

Knowing now he really was a member of the family.

"I will wash you off." Wendy said, "Then we will talk about this some more over a nice cup of tea.

I hope you are not too mad at me."

After Tickles was clean,
Wendy sat Tickles down at the Tea Party and said,
"Tickles I was not trying to be mean.
I dropped you in the forest,
But I was scared, and I did not know I lost you, of course!
Can you still be my friend?"
"Yes," Tickles said, "but it would be best if we never went into the forest again!"

"Agreed!" Wendy said.

She picked Tickles up to get him ready for bed.

"You must be cold and tired. You need to rest."

Tickles felt that Wendy was very thoughtful. She was the best!

Wendy gave Tickles one last big hug.

She placed Tickles in bed and made him all snug.

He was now safe and warm at the end of the day.

Tickles thought, "Tomorrow will be another fun day to play!"

Pizza Contest

Wendy Feldoon was not a very fast eater— so they say,
She could start eating a cookie and make it last the whole day!
Today the Feldoons went to the County Fair.
Wendy told Tickles there were lots of fun things to see and do there.
Wendy and Tickles went on every ride.
They were all getting hungry, now, and could smell something delicious being fried.
Wendy saw a sign. "Free Pizza This Way! Enter the Pizza Eating Contest, at noon, today!"

Wendy had just been given a watch. She had just learned how to tell time. It was 11:49!

Wendy asked her parents if she could enter the contest. Her parents said that would be just fine.

Wendy was excited to enter the Pizza Contest,

But Tickles confessed,

"I do not care for pizza. I like blueberry pie the best!"

Her parents wondered if Wendy would ever be able to eat fast enough.

To win a pizza contest required you to eat pizza as fast as you could until you were stuffed!

Wendy was hungry and she wanted to try.

She sat down next to a rather large looking guy.

His name was Ivan Injester. He could eat a lot.
Ivan looked over at Wendy. "I will have no problem eating more than her!" he thought.
Next to Ivan was Valerie Vacyum and next to Valerie was Marty Munchase.
Frankly, Wendy looked a little out of place.
The others were veterans. They had entered many pizza contests before.
They knew how to win. They always came back to win some more.
"The rules for the pizza contest are quite simple. Eat as much pizza as fast as you can."
Said the pizza contest judge. His name was Dan.

The pizzas were brought to each contestant and Wendy looked down.

There were twelve pieces of pizza. It looked quite good. The crust was perfect— a light brown.

"Twelve pieces of pizza like the numbers on a clock."

Wendy thought, "Each piece of pizza I will number like a tick tock!"

Ivan looked at Wendy, as he ate his first piece.

He thought, "I will win this contest with ease!"

Wendy continued to think of the pizza as a clock. She looked at Ivan and told him it was not polite to gawk!

Wendy thought, "Each number on a clock is five minutes. Twelve pieces of pizza, five minutes a piece,
Sixty seconds a minute— that is three hundred nibbles of pizza a piece, if you please!
A nibble a second is what I will do!
It will take me an hour to eat this pizza. I will have to use all my power to chew!"
She took off her watch and set it down on the table.
Wendy picked up a piece. She was ready and able.
She said "Three hundred nibbles a piece.
I am ready to feast!"

The other contestants had all eaten at least two
pieces by then.
In no time at all the contest would end!
The crowd was cheering and encouraging the
contestants to eat.
Tickles the Bear was so excited he was standing on
his seat!
Valerie Vacyum looked over at Wendy.
She wanted to know how many pieces of pizza
Wendy had eaten. She saw that it was not many.
Valerie saw Wendy's watch and she saw Wendy
nibble.
Valerie dropped her pizza and she started to giggle.

Her parents, in the audience, frowned.

They knew that once Valerie started giggling they would not hear another sound.

For hours Valerie would be laughing, now.

Her parents said, "When she wants to stop laughing she does not know how!"

Marty Munchase had picked up his sixth piece.

He was starting to eat it but Valerie was laughing at something and she would not cease!

Marty looked over at Wendy with pizza sauce oozing out both sides of his mouth.

Wendy was nibbling, every second, like a little mouse.

Marty could not help himself. He started to laugh.

He laughed so hard he started choking. Marty had to stop eating pizza— after only finishing half.

Ivan was still eating. He was determined to win.
Ten pieces! Eleven pieces! Wendy's chance to win was growing thin!
Ivan was a little disturbed by all the laughing and choking.
He thought the reason was because Wendy was joking!
Ivan looked over at Wendy and he could not believe what he saw.
He let out a big guffaw!
Wendy was not nearly done.
He said to himself, "This will be fun!"
Ivan stuffed the last piece of pizza in his mouth.
With both of his hands, he stuffed it all in—
Thinking that was all he needed to do to win.

The judge ran over to Ivan and tried to explain,
"To win the contest, right now, you must
completely swallow the pizza that is in your
mouth!"

Ivan looked like he was in great pain.

Ivan had stuffed too much pizza in his mouth. He
could not swallow.

There was no way he could win. He turned his back
to the crowd and let out a big bellow!

That was it! Wendy could now easily win.

She took a nibble a second until sixty nibbles were
done.

Sixty nibbles was sixty seconds or a minute to you.

Each piece of pizza took five minutes to chew.

On the clock, the long hand passed the number one and when she finished the second piece the long hand passed the number two.

Tickles fell asleep at nibble number eighteen hundred and ninety two!

Wendy's parents cheered her on. She was done! Wendy nibbled thirty six hundred nibbles and won! An hour of nibbling pizza— in sixty minutes she had finished it all.

Twelve pieces of pizza later, her prize was a beautiful doll!

Snow!

Tickles woke up. It was another fine day.
He was ready to play just like on every other day.
Wendy was away at a place called school.
It was not for bears, although Tickles was no fool.
He had learned a lot from Wendy and Wendy's
parents too! Tickles could count to ten.
He could recite rhymes. He could draw circles,
squares and triangles with a pen.
Up Tickles rose from his bed on that day,
He walked to a window exactly ten steps away.
Some soft, white, fluffy stuff was falling from the
sky.
"Yippee, Yahoo!" is what came next out of this cute
little guy.

"It is snowing!" he said.

"It is time to go out and sled!"

Tickles remembered the time he was supposed to stay inside, at Santa's, but went outside instead.

Tickles went to see Snowball. Snowball was now assigned to take care of Miss Sneeza—

The beautiful doll that Wendy won eating pizza.

"A beautiful doll!" Wendy had said. She was really quite pleased.

Wendy, later, named the doll Miss Sneeza because, as beautiful as she was, she continually sneezed!

"Kerchoo!" she would say and daintily wipe her nose.

I must have allergies to all these furry animals, I suppose.

Snowball did not have fur. He was feathery to the touch.

Snowball did notice that when Tickles was not around she did not sneeze— quite so much.

Snowball had to make sure Miss Sneeza was alright.

He had to fetch plenty of tissue for Miss Sneeza to use at night.

Tickles went over to Snowball and greeted Miss Sneeza with a "How do you do?"

"A little chilly today." she said and let out a dainty "Kerchoo!"

"Snowball," Tickles said, "It is snowing outside! I don't know about you but I am ready to slide!"

Snowball said, "Well, that is all very fine.
But first, a box to use and then a hill we must find."
"Perhaps this tissue box will do."
Said Miss Sneeza, "Kerchoo!"
"Excellent choice!" said Snowball, "It will fit you
and me!"
"It is large enough for you, me and Miss Sneeza."
Tickles said, quite proudly, "It will fit all three!
How do we get outside?
I am ready to ride!"

Snowball said, "I do not know. We are upstairs and inside. We must somehow get downstairs, outside, and into the snow."

Tickles said, "I have an idea! We can slide down the stairs in this box!"

"Better leave some tissue in the bottom," Snowball said. "It will soften the bumps and the knocks!"

So with a push and a shove, Tickles, Miss Sneeza, and Snowball slid down the stairs from above.

Snowball and Tickles yelled, "Yahoo! Yippee!"

Miss Sneeza sang a single note from an opera melody.

Tickles thought her singing was quite pretty.

Right then, Wendy opened the front door.

Wendy was surprised at what she saw on the floor.

She saw Tickles and two more!

They were all ready to go

Outside and into the snow!

It was a perfect day to slide down a hill and yell

"Yahoo!"

Wendy was ready too!

Toby

It was Tickles' days and Tickles' nights.
Wendy played with Tickles day after day without any fights.
But then it happened. Things were not the same.
Tickles wanted to play with Wendy. Wendy never came.
She spent all of her time downstairs.
Tickles felt bad. He said, "Wendy no longer cares."

What was downstairs that kept Wendy away?
Tickles wondered, "Why hasn't Wendy come to play with me at all today?"
So out of the bedroom Tickles did go.
Tickles just knew it was the right thing to do.
He slid down the stairs using a flat part of the stair's railing.
By the time Tickles hit the ground floor he was really sailing!

He tumbled and he flipped quite far along the floor.
When he finally stopped he said to himself,
"That was fun! I am ready to slide down the stairs some more!"
Tickles stood up. He was starting to look around.
When, all of a sudden, it hit with a sharp, barking sound.
Tickles found he was being licked, all over, from head to toe.
Wendy had just bought a brand, new puppy, you know.

Wendy was quick to follow the puppy's sound.
She found Tickles all wet from puppy kisses lying on the ground.
She said, "Oh Tickles, I bet this is a big surprise.
I will have to introduce you to my new puppy so we can play together.
I love you two cute, little guys!"
So in the end things were all the same.
Wendy played with Tickles but let her puppy in on the game.

Tickles told Wendy the puppy was quite well behaved— quite tame.

Wendy agreed, but frowned a little. She said she still had not picked out a name.

Tickles said, "Do not worry. You will figure out a name for your puppy.

You will know when it is meant TO BE."

Wendy's eyes lit up. It was the right choice, you see,

To name her dog from what Tickles had just said.

"I will name him Toby!"

Sing A Song!

Tickles and Snowball were standing around one day
Not knowing quite what to play.
Tickles said,
"Do you think it is rude
To talk about food?
When we were eating some crunchy cookies, one day,
I did not quite hear what Wendy had to say."

Snowball said, "You did not hear her quite right.
She probably said that it was not polite
To talk with your mouth full of food.
It is not a pretty sight
And it is considered quite rude."

"Hey!

I know what we can play!

Let's make up a song about food. What do you say?"

"Yes!" Tickles said, "You go first and I will go second.

It will take me some time to think up a song, I reckon."

Snowball said, "I will make up a song about spaghetti.

Here I go. Are you ready?"

"I love spaghetti in the morning.

I love noodles at noon.

I love lasagna.

I love ricotta.

I hope I get some pasta real soon!"

Tickles snickered and he giggled.

He laughed so hard his ears wiggled.

"That was a nice song, Snowball.

You thought of it in no time at all!

Now it is my turn to make up a song. I will try!"

Tickles said, "I will try and sing a song about pie!"

"I love pie! It's a tasty, scrumptious treat—
Fruity too and juicy sweet!
Blackberry, Blueberry,
Raisin, Apple, Peach!
Please give me one of each!"

They marched along—
Each singing their song.
It was a fun way to pass the day.
Singing songs about food was OK!
But Tickles learned that it would be considered
quite rude
If he we were to start singing with a mouth full of
food.

<u>Feet!</u>

Tickles and Snowball were sitting around one day.

They were looking at their feet.

They did not know what to play.

Tickles said, "Your feet are kind of flippy and

floppy and neat!

I would like to have toes like the ones on your

feet!"

Snowball said, "I believe the proper term for your feet are paws.
It comes from a long line of papa bears. Yes it does!
If you had my feet you would look like a duck—
Except with fur. They would be good in the muck!"
Tickles explained as he pondered it,
"It would be nice to have toes. I could watch them wiggle."
Wendy walked in and she started to giggle.

Wendy said, as she was deciding where she would sit, "You can watch my toes wiggle!"
She sat down and gave them each one small tickle.
Wendy took off her shoes and her socks from her feet.
She wiggled her toes on one foot and then the other.
Then she wiggled all ten toes together.
Tickles and Snowball thought that was pretty neat!

Wendy said, "Enjoy what you have because it is all
you will get.
We each have two feet. They come in a set.
If you were me and I was you.
It would not make us any better,
Because I love you two!
I am just happy that we are all together!

Friends From Far Away

Wendy ran out of the house and started to cry.
She saw Tickles and Snowball in a big shoe, tied to balloons, way up in the sky.
She said, "I love you my bear. Please come down from way up there!"
Tickles shouted, "I do not know what to do!
I do not know how to steer this shoe!"
So Tickles and Snowball went up and away.
They went floating over the city at the end of day.
"Do not worry. Wendy will think of something." Snowball said.
Snowball looked way down to the ground and started to feel a little dizzy in his head.

It was not Wendy that would rescue Tickles. It was an elf—
The mischievous elf that had made Tickles, himself.
A thread of fear was pulling at the elf's heart.
The elf knew that Wendy and Tickles were apart!
He ran to tell Santa. He did not know where to start.
"Santa there is something wrong with a bear I made named Tickles, I feel.
A part of my elf magic must have seeped in and made him real.
Now he is in trouble. Where? I do not know.
I can feel the threads of his fear tugging inside me from my head to my toe!"

Santa's brow frowned, his nose started to wrinkle.
But in his eyes, there was still a small twinkle.
There was silence in the air.
The elf started to shiver under Santa's intense stare.
But Santa was only thinking.
When he came up with a plan his eyes really started twinkling!

Santa said, "Ah yes, Tickles is Wendy's bear.
She is a kind little girl that really does care!
Let us go and take a look.
We will scan the skyways and byways,
We will look for Tickles in every nook and crook!"
Santa took the elf up and away.
It did not take them long to find Tickles in Santa's sleigh.

Santa said, "Ho! Ho! Ho! There they are!"
It was getting late and Tickles was looking at the night's first star.
With a twitch of his nose and at the speed of light, Santa picked up Tickles and Snowball.
He brought them back to Wendy's house on that night.
It happened so fast that no one can really say
How Tickles and Snowball ended up back at Wendy's house on that day.
The mischievous elf, in a magical minute, tied a bright red bow
Around the big shoe's toe!

Wendy was outside still crying. She turned around.
Wendy was going back to the house to tell her parent's the bad news—
But there, on the ground,
She saw Tickles and Snowball in a big shoe—
wouldn't you know!
The shoe had a ribbon tied around it in a bright red bow!
Wendy blinked twice. Her eyes were still full of tears.
Her heart was pounding and her mind was full of fears.

Wendy knelt down and picked both of them up
from the shoe.
She gave Tickles and Snowball several big hugs and
said,
"I do not know what I am going to do with you two!
I thought you were way up in the air.
I thought you were in great danger up there."

Tickles was not sure how they returned to the ground just then.

But he was very happy their high flying adventures were at an end.

Snowball might have known, he said "It is good to have friends in far away places!"

Tickles looked at Snowball and started to make funny faces!

Tickles made a funny face at Snowball and Snowball made a funny face back.

Tickles said, "I do not know about you but I am starving and in need of a tasty, nighttime snack!"

As Wendy walked to the house she began singing a

song.

She had had been singing the song all day long.

"This is the bear that I care for.

This is the bear I adore.

In this whole world there is no bear

That I can say I love more."

About the Author

Marcel lives with his wife and two daughters on Cougar Mountain, near Seattle, Washington.

www.ingramcontent.com/pod-product-compliance
Lightning Source LLC
Chambersburg PA
CBHW031414040426
42444CB00005B/557